BRAZIL

Alice Harman

WAYLAND

FACT CAT

Get your paws on this fantastic new mega-series from Wayland!

Join our Fact Cat on a journey of fun learning about every subject under the sun!

First published in 2014 by Wayland
© Wayland 2014

Wayland
Hachette Children's Books
338 Euston Road
London NW1 3BH

Wayland Australia
Level 17/207 Kent Street
Sydney NSW 2000

 Produced for Wayland by
White-Thomson Publishing Ltd
www.wtpub.co.uk
+44 (0) 843 208 7460

Editor: Alice Harman/Izzi Howell
Design: Rocket Design (East Anglia) Ltd
Fact Cat illustrations: Shutterstock/Julien Troneur
Other illustrations: Stefan Chabluk
Consultant: Kate Ruttle

A catalogue for this title is available from the British Library

ISBN: 978 0 7502 8213 0
ebook ISBN: 978 0 7502 8826 2

Dewey Number: 981-dc23

10 9 8 7 6 5 4 3 2 1

Wayland is a division of Hachette Children's Books,
an Hachette UK company.
www.hachette.co.uk

Printed and bound in China

Picture and illustration credits:
Alamy: Robert Harding cover, BrazilPhotos.com 9;
Chabluk, Stefan: 4; Dreamstime: Mypix 6, Sfmthd 11,
Carlos Mora 13, Frank Schoen 15, Pixattitude 17, Lazyllama
18; Photoshot: TTL 7; Shutterstock: Procy 10, Celso Pupo
16, CREATISTA 19, Kostas Koutsaftikis 20; Thinkstock:
Sohadiszno/iStock 8, Igor Alecsander/iStock 12, lightpoet
14; Wikimedia: Agencia Brazil 21.

Every effort has been made to clear copyright.
Should there be any inadvertent omission,
please apply to the publisher for rectification.

The author, Alice Harman, is a writer and editor specialising in children's educational publishing.

The consultant, Kate Ruttle, is a literacy expert and SENCO, and teaches in Suffolk.

FACT CAT FACT

There is a question for you to answer on each spread in this book. You can check your answers on page 24.

CONTENTS

WELCOME TO BRAZIL

Brazil is a country in South America. It is the fifth largest country in the world. Around 200 million people live there.

Brazilians speak Portuguese. Find out which language people speak in other South American countries.

Brasília is the **capital** city of Brazil. Around 2.8 million people live there, which makes it the fourth largest city in Brazil.

Brasília was built around 55 years ago. Brazil's leaders wanted to create a new capital city with lots of **modern** buildings and parks.

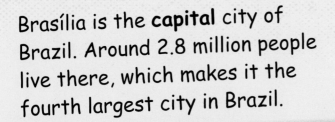

FACT CAT FACT

The Amazon River is the widest river in the world. If you stand on one side of it, you often can't see the land on the other side!

CITIES

Most people in Brazil live in cities. There are thousands of cities and towns in Brazil. The largest city is São Paulo, where more than 11 million people live.

Rio de Janeiro is Brazil's second biggest city. Brazilians call it *La Cidade Maravilhosa* (the marvellous city) because of its beautiful **landscape**.

FACT CAT FACT

Many people in Brazil's cities live in *favelas*. These are poor, crowded areas with badly built houses.

In Salvador, women dressed in traditional outfits sell food outside. Acarajés are the most popular street food. Try to find out how they are made.

There are large cities all over Brazil. Manaus and Belém are both beside the River Amazon. Salvador, Fortaleza and Recife are along the north-east coast.

COUNTRYSIDE

Brazil has many different types of landscape. There are mountains, large areas of **rainforest** and **wetland**, deserts, grassy **plains** and wide sandy beaches.

Chapada Diamantina is a **national park** in the state of Bahia. Brazil has 26 states. Can you find out the names of three more?

There are many small towns and villages in the countryside. People there often work as farmers or in tourism. Some people also live in villages in the forest.

Traditional **tribes** of Brazilian people have often lived in the same area for thousands of years. They hunt, fish and pick fruit and vegetables for food.

FACT CAT FACT

There are at least 67 tribes in Brazil who have no contact with the rest of the world. Some people want to chop down their forest, and sell the wood or land. Others help to protect the forest and the tribes.

SIGHTS

Many people come to Brazil to see its amazing natural sights. The Iguazu Falls are 275 different waterfalls that fall in one area on the Iguazu River.

The Iguazu Falls are partly in Brazil and partly in another country. Try to find out which other country this is.

Christ the Redeemer is a huge statue of Jesus Christ in Rio de Janeiro. It stands on the top of Corcovado Mountain, looking over the city below. Many tourists come to visit it.

The statue was built around 85 years ago. It weighs 635 tonnes, which is as heavy as 127 elephants!

FOOD AND DRINK

Many people in Brazil eat rice and beans every day, either with meat or fish. Each area of Brazil also has its own special foods. By the coast, seafood **stews** are popular.

Brazil's most famous dish is feijoada. It is a stew of pork, beef and black beans. It is often eaten with rice and sprinkled with crunchy flour called **farofa**.

FACT CAT FACT

In the area of Brazil around the Amazon River, people often eat piranha fish. Piranhas sometimes **attack** humans, but they mostly use their sharp teeth to bite other fish!

Many different fruits and vegetables grow in Brazil. People drink fresh juices made from fruits such as mango, **passion fruit** and pineapple.

There are many Brazilian fruits that you may never have seen before. Try to find out what jaca, guaraná, caju and pitanga fruits look like.

WILDLIFE

A lot of Brazil's wildlife is found in the rainforest along the Amazon River. Many of the animals don't live anywhere else on Earth. A new animal or plant is found there about every three days.

Squirrel monkeys eat fruit, insects and small animals. Find out the names of two other animals in the Amazon rainforest, and see what they eat.

Many Brazilian animals also live in the Pantanal. This is the largest area of wetland in the world. When there is lots of rain, the rivers flood the grassy plains so there are islands of land.

Jaguars hunt on land and in the water. They eat **caiman**, wild pigs, monkeys, deer, fish, birds and turtles.

FACT CAT FACT

More than 100,000 different types of animals live in the Amazon rainforest. Most of these are minibeasts. However, the rainforest and its animals may disappear soon if people don't stop chopping down so much of it.

FESTIVALS

Carnaval is a huge celebration that lasts for four days. People watch exciting parades of dancers wearing colourful costumes. The biggest parties are in Rio de Janeiro, Salvador and Olinda.

Carnaval takes place in the spring, but its exact date changes each year. Can you find out what date it is this year?

Festivals around Brazil celebrate the traditions of different areas. At Parintins Folklore Festival, two teams try to tell the best version of a local story about an **ox**.

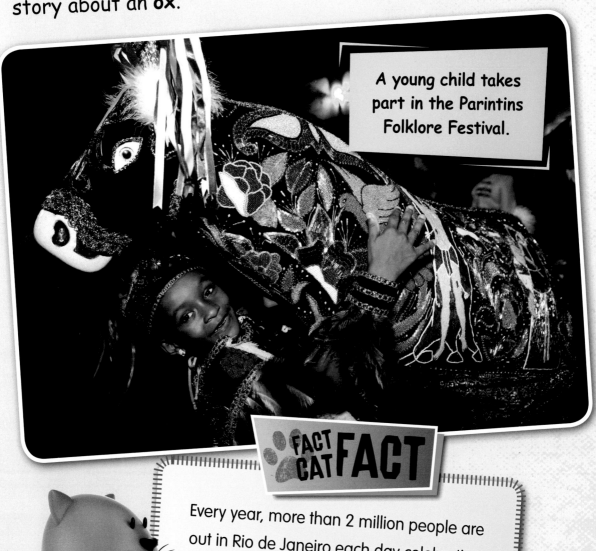

A young child takes part in the Parintins Folklore Festival.

FACT CAT FACT

Every year, more than 2 million people are out in Rio de Janeiro each day celebrating Carnaval. This makes the Rio Carnaval the biggest party in the world!

SPORT

Three of the most popular Brazilian sports are football, volleyball and basketball. Brazil's men's and women's football teams are among the best in the world.

Footvolley is a game that was created in Brazil around 40 years ago. It is a mixture of football and volleyball, and is a very popular beach game. Players use both their feet and hands.

Millions of people all over Brazil play and watch football. Can you find out how many times the men's football team has won the **World Cup**?

Martial arts are also very popular in Brazil. Many people like mixed martial arts and Brazilian jiu-jitsu. Capoeira is a martial art that includes music, dance and **acrobatics**.

The first people in Brazil to do capoeira were **slaves** who were brought over from Africa. It helped them to practise fighting while they seemed to be dancing.

FAMOUS PEOPLE

Pelé is a famous **retired** Brazilian footballer.
His real name is Edson Arantes do Nascimento.
Many people think he is the
greatest footballer of all time.

Pelé scored more goals
during his career than
any other footballer.
Can you find out how
many goals he scored?

SECURITY
PRIVATE

FACT CAT FACT

Pele grew up in a very poor family in
São Paulo, and his dad taught him
to play football. He could not afford a
football, so he played with a grapefruit
or a sock stuffed with newspaper.

Dilma Rousseff became the first female **president** of Brazil in 2011. When she was much younger, she went to jail for fighting against the people who ruled Brazil.

Rousseff was in jail for three years, and she was treated very badly there. She carried on fighting when she left jail, and became a **politician**.

Try to answer the questions below. Look back through the book to help you. Check your answers on page 24.

1 Brazilians speak Spanish. True or not true?

a) true

b) not true

2 How many people live in São Paulo?

a) 5 million

b) 11 million

c) 13 million

3 The city of Manaus is built on which river?

a) Amazon

b) Ganges

c) Nile

4 The statue of Christ the Redeemer looks over which city?

a) Salvador

b) Brasília

c) Rio de Janeiro

5 What is farofa?

a) flour for cooking

b) a dance

c) a musical instrument

6 The Brazilians are not good at football. True or not true?

a) true

b) not true

GLOSSARY

acrobatics when someone does exciting jumping and balancing tricks

attack to fight and hurt someone/something

caiman an animal that lives in the Amazon River that is like a small crocodile

capital the city where the government meets to make the laws of the country

farofa a toasted flour mixture

flood when there is a flood, a lot of water spreads over the land

hunt to chase and kill animals

island a piece of land with water all around it

landscape everything you can see when you look out over an area of land

martial arts fighting sports such as judo and karate

minibeasts very small creatures

modern something that uses new ideas and styles

national park an area where the landscape and wildlife are protected by the law

ox an animal like a cow

passion fruit a juicy tropical fruit

plains large areas of flat ground

politician a person who works for the government of a country

president someone who rules a country

rainforest a thick forest where there are heavy rains almost every day

retired no longer working

slave someone who works hard for little pay and is controlled by another person

stews a mixture of meat or vegetables cooked in a sauce

tourist someone who visits a place on holiday

traditional the way that people have done things for a long time

tribe a group of people who live together and are ruled by a chief

wetland an area of land that is covered by shallow water

World Cup a football competition that is held every four years in which thirty two countries compete to win the Cup

INDEX

ANSWERS

Pages 4–20

page 4: Portuguese

page 7: black-eyed peas are made into a ball and deep fried in palm oil

page 8: Espírito Santo, Amazonas, Mato Grosso

page 10: Argentina

page 14: Sloth, eats leaves from trees; armadillo, eats insects and especially likes ants

page 20: 1,281 goals

Quiz answers

1   b) Not true.
    They speak Portuguese.

2   b) 11 million

3   a) Amazon

4   c) Rio de Janeiro

5   a) flour for cooking

6   b) Not true.
    Brazil has won the World Cup five times, more than any other country.

OTHER TITLES IN THE FACT CAT SERIES...

SPACE

978 0 7502 8221 5

978 0 7502 8223 9

978 0 7502 8222 2

978 0 7502 8220 8

UNITED KINGDOM

978 0 7502 8433 2

978 0 7502 8439 4

978 0 7502 8440 0

978 0 7502 8438 7

HISTORY

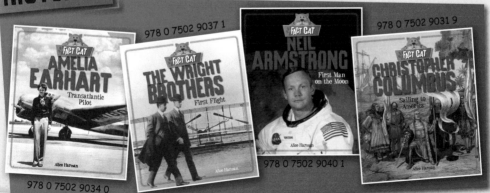

978 0 7502 9037 1

978 0 7502 9031 9

978 0 7502 9040 1

978 0 7502 9034 0

WAYLAND